EAT UP, GEMMA

Written by
Sarah Hayes

Illustrated by
Jan Ormerod

Here's all the great literature in this grade level of *Celebrate Reading!*

The Doorbell Rang
by Pat Hutchins

ONE GORILLA
Atsuko Morozumi

THE NEW YORK TIMES
BEST ILLUSTRATED CHILDREN'S BOOK AWARD
WINNER

Under My Hat

Finding a Starting Point

Big Books & Little Books

It's a Perfect Day!
by Abigail Pizer
✳ CHILDREN'S CHOICE AUTHOR

Peanut Butter and Jelly
Illustrations by
Nadine Bernard Westcott
✳ CHILDREN'S CHOICE ILLUSTRATOR

The Gunnywolf
retold and illustrated
by A. Delaney
✳ CHILDREN'S CHOICE

So Can I
by Allan Ahlberg
✳ CHILDREN'S BOOK AWARD AUTHOR

One Gorilla
by Atsuko Morozumi
✳ NEW YORK TIMES BEST ILLUSTRATED

Mary Had a Little Lamb
by Sarah Josepha Hale
Photographs by
Bruce McMillan
✳ ALA NOTABLE ILLUSTRATOR

David McCord

BOOK B

Hurry, Furry Feet

Old Hat, New Hat
by Stan and Jan Berenstain
❋ MICHIGAN YOUNG READER
AWARD AUTHORS

The Foot Book and
Hurry, Hurry, Hurry
by Dr. Seuss
❋ CALDECOTT HONOR ILLUSTRATOR
❋ LAURA INGALLS WILDER AWARD
AUTHOR/ILLUSTRATOR

My Street Begins at My House
by Ella Jenkins
Illustrations by
James E. Ransome
❋ PARENTS' CHOICE SONGWRITER

When the Elephant Walks
by Keiko Kasza
❋ ALA NOTABLE AUTHOR

Sitting in My Box
by Dee Lillegard
Illustrations by Jon Agee
❋ NEW YORK TIMES BEST ILLUSTRATOR

Featured Poet

Evelyn Beyer

Big Book & Little Book

The Wheels on the Bus
by Maryann Kovalski

BOOK C
Our Singing Planet

"Pardon?" Said the Giraffe
by Colin West

I Can Make Music
by Eve B. Feldman

The Little Red Hen and the Grain of Wheat
by Sara Cone Bryant

My Mom Travels a Lot
by Caroline Feller Bauer
Illustrations by
Nancy Winslow Parker
✷ CHRISTOPHER AWARD
✷ NEW YORK TIMES BEST ILLUSTRATED

Tommy Meng San
by Belinda Yun-Ying
and Douglas Louie

Featured Poets

N. M. Bodecker
Rowena Bennett
Mary Ann Hoberman
Lee Bennett Hopkins

Big Book & Little Book

No Puppies Today!
by Joanna Cole
Illustrations by Brian Karas
✷ ALA NOTABLE AUTHOR
✷ CHILDREN'S CHOICE AUTHOR
✷ TEACHERS' CHOICE AUTHOR

BOOK D
My Favorite Foodles

The Doorbell Rang
by Pat Hutchins
✳ ALA NOTABLE CHILDREN'S BOOK
✳ CHILDREN'S CHOICE

Aiken Drum
Traditional Song

**The Great, Big,
Enormous Turnip**
retold by Alexei Tolstoy
Illustrations by
Helen Oxenbury
✳ ALA NOTABLE ILLUSTRATOR
✳ KATE GREENAWAY MEDAL
ILLUSTRATOR

From Seeds to Zucchinis
by LuLu Delacre

Hello, House!
retold by Linda Hayward
Illustrations by
Lynn Munsinger
✳ NEW YORK TIMES BEST ILLUSTRATOR
✳ CHILDREN'S CHOICE

Featured Poets

Eve Merriam
Lucia and James L. Hymes, Jr.
Dennis Lee
John Ciardi
Charlotte Zolotow

Big Book & Little Book

If You Give a Moose a Muffin
by Laura Joffe Numeroff
Illustrations by Felicia Bond
✳ CHILDREN'S CHOICE

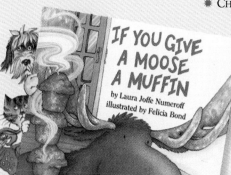

BOOK E
Happy Faces

Mouse's Marriage
by Junko Morimoto
✳ AUSTRALIAN PICTURE BOOK
OF THE YEAR ILLUSTRATOR

Who Will Bell the Cat?
retold as a play
by Sandy Asher

The Mice Go Marching
by Hap Palmer
✳ PARENTS' CHOICE SONGWRITER

Mama's Birthday Present
by Carmen Tafolla

Baby Rattlesnake
told by TeAta
retold by Lynn Moroney

The Desert
by Carol Carrick
✳ NEW YORK TIMES NOTABLE AUTHOR

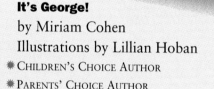

It's George!
by Miriam Cohen
Illustrations by Lillian Hoban
✳ CHILDREN'S CHOICE AUTHOR
✳ PARENTS' CHOICE AUTHOR
✳ CHRISTOPHER AWARD ILLUSTRATOR

Featured Poets

Eloise Greenfield
Karla Kuskin
Myra Cohn Livingston

Big Book & Little Book

On the Go
by Ann Morris
Photographs by Ken Heyman

BOOK F

A Canary with Hiccups

Two Greedy Bears
retold by Mirra Ginsburg
Illustrations by
Jose Aruego and Ariane Dewey
✳ ALA NOTABLE AUTHOR
✳ BOSTON GLOBE-HORN
BOOK AWARD ILLUSTRATORS

Eat Up, Gemma
by Sarah Hayes
Illustrations by Jan Ormerod
✳ KATE GREENAWAY
AUTHOR/ILLUSTRATOR TEAM AWARD

A Healthy Day
by Paul Showers
✳ NEW JERSEY INSTITUTE OF
TECHNOLOGY AWARD AUTHOR

Looby Loo
Traditional Song

**Henry and Mudge
and the Forever Sea**
from the story by
Cynthia Rylant
Illustrations by Suçie Stevenson
✳ PARENTING READING MAGIC AWARD
✳ NEWBERY MEDAL AUTHOR

Amazing Pets
by Lynda DeWitt

Fox on the Job
from the story by
James Marshall
✳ ALA NOTABLE CHILDREN'S AUTHOR
✳ READING RAINBOW SELECTION

Do Your Ears Hang Low?
Illustrations by Lois Ehlert
✳ ALA NOTABLE ILLUSTRATOR

Ready...Set...Read!
from the book by Joanna Cole
and Stephanie Calmenson
Illustrations by Lois Ehlert

Featured Poets

Jack Prelutsky
Lee Bennett Hopkins
Shel Silverstein
Gail Kredenser
Zheyna Gay

Big Book & Little Book

The Goat Who Couldn't Sneeze
retold by Cecilia Avalos
Illustrations by Vivi Escrivá

Celebrate Reading!
Big Book Bonus

It Looked Like Spilt Milk
by Charles G. Shaw

Jamberry
by Bruce Degen
✳ CHILDREN'S CHOICE

Skip to My Lou
by Nadine Bernard Westcott
✳ REDBOOK CHILDREN'S
PICTURE BOOK AWARD

Lazy Lion
by Mwenye Hadithi
Illustrations by
Adrienne Kennaway
✳ KATE GREENAWAY MEDAL
ILLUSTRATOR

The Cake That Mack Ate
by Rose Robart
Illustrations by
Maryann Kovalski

The Right Number of Elephants
by Jeff Sheppard

A Canary with Hiccups

Titles in This Set

Under My Hat

Hurry, Furry Feet

Our Singing Planet

My Favorite Foodles

Happy Faces

A Canary with Hiccups

About the Cover

The picture on the cover was painted by Michele Noiset.
She loves to draw animals that are playful and funny.
Ms. Noiset began drawing when she was very young.
Her grandfather, an artist, gave her lots of encouragement.

ISBN: 0-673-81126-3

1997
Scott, Foresman and Company, Glenview, Illinois
All Rights Reserved.
Printed in the United States of America.

Acknowledgments appear on page 128.

45678910DQ0100999897

A Canary with Hiccups

ScottForesman

Contents

Bears–Oh My!

Two Greedy Bears 10
Hungarian folk tale retold by Mirra Ginsburg
Illustrations by Jose Aruego and Ariane Dewey

A Word from the Illustrators 39
Article by Jose Aruego and Ariane Dewey

Polar Bear 40
Poem by Gail Kredenser

In the Summer We Eat 41
Poem by Zhenya Gay

Happy and Healthy

Eat Up, Gemma   44

Realistic fiction by Sarah Hayes

Illustrations by Jan Ormerod

A Healthy Day   68

Expository nonfiction by Paul Showers

A Word from the Author   75

Article by Paul Showers

Looby Loo   76

Traditional song

This Tooth   80

Poem by Lee Bennett Hopkins

Pets

"Brave Dog"   **84**

from *Henry and Mudge and the Forever Sea*

Realistic fiction by Cynthia Rylant

Illustrations by Suçie Stevenson

Amazing Pets   **96**

Expository nonfiction by Lynda DeWitt

The Lost Cat   **102**

Poem by Shel Silverstein

My Fish Can Ride a Bicycle   **103**

Poem by Jack Prelutsky

Illustration by James Stevenson

Something Funny

"Pizza Time"   106
from *Fox on the Job*
Fantasy written and illustrated by James Marshall

Do Your Ears Hang Low?   118
Traditional song
Illustration by Lois Ehlert

A Riddle   119
by Joanna Cole and Stephanie Calmenson
Illustration by Lois Ehlert

Student Resources
Books to Enjoy   120
Glossary   122

Bears—Oh My!

9

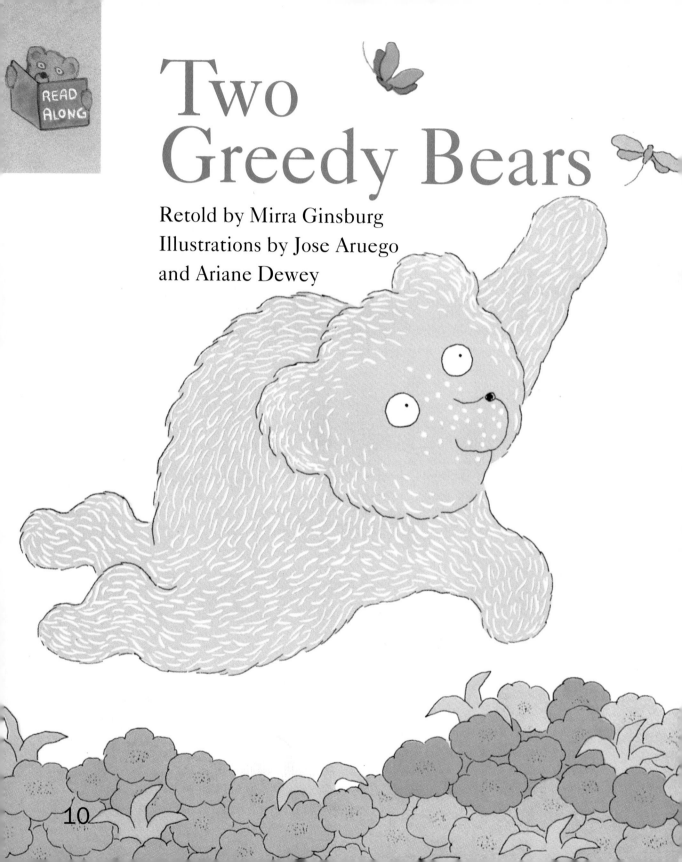

Two Greedy Bears

Retold by Mirra Ginsburg

Illustrations by Jose Aruego
and Ariane Dewey

Two bear cubs went out to see the world.

They walked and walked, till they came to a brook.

"I'm thirsty," said one.
"I'm thirstier," said the other.

They put their heads down to the water and drank.

"You had more," cried one, and drank some more.
"Now you had more," cried the other, and drank
   some more.

And so they drank and drank,
and their stomachs got bigger and bigger,
till a frog peeked out of the water and laughed.

"Look at those pot-bellied bear cubs! If they drink any more they'll burst!"

The bear cubs sat down on the grass
and looked at their stomachs.

"I have a stomach ache," one cried.
"I have a bigger one," cried the other.
    They cried and cried, till they fell asleep.

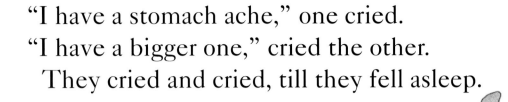

In the morning they woke up feeling better
and continued their journey.

"I am hungry," said one.
"I am hungrier," said the other.

21

And suddenly they saw a big round cheese lying by the roadside. They wanted to divide it. But they did not know how to break it into equal parts. Each was afraid the other would get the bigger piece.

24

They argued, and they growled, and they began to fight, till a fox came by.

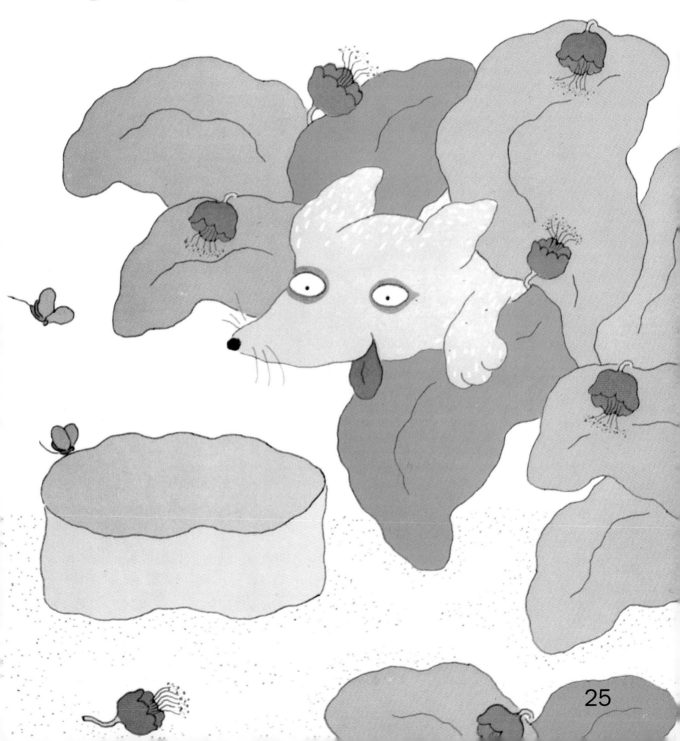

25

"What are you arguing about?" the sly one
   asked the bear cubs.
"We don't know how to divide the cheese
   so that we'll both get equal parts."
"That's easy," she said. "I'll help you."

28

She took the cheese and broke it in two.
But she made sure that one piece was bigger
than the other, and the bear cubs cried,
"That one is bigger!"

"Don't worry. I know what to do."
   And she took a big bite out of the larger piece.
"Now that one's bigger!"

"Have patience!" And she
   took a bite out of the second piece.
"Now this one's bigger!"

"Wait, wait," the fox said with her mouth full of cheese. "In just a moment they'll be equal." She took another bite, and then another.

34

And the bear cubs kept turning their black noses
from the bigger piece to the smaller one,
from the smaller one to the bigger one.
"Now this one's bigger!"
"Now that one's bigger!"

35

And the fox kept on dividing and dividing
the cheese, till she could eat no more.
"And now, good appetite to you, my friends!"
She flicked her tail and stalked away.

By then all that was left of the big round
cheese were two tiny crumbs.
But they were equal!

Our Greedy Bears

by Jose Aruego and Ariane Dewey

I drew the bears for Two Greedy Bears. I copied them
from the bears I pictured in my mind. That way they
were MY bears. Then I went to a museum to see if my
bears looked like the real thing … and, in many ways,
they did!!!

Jose Aruego

I painted Jose's drawings bright colors. Bears love honey,
so I made one of the bears honey-colored. To make
them look furry, I covered them with hundreds
of brush strokes. They're greedy but lovable bears.

Ariane Dewey

39

Polar Bear

by Gail Kredenser

The secret of the polar bear
Is that he wears long underwear.

In the Summer We Eat

by Zhenya Gay

In the summer we eat,
In the winter we don't;
In the summer we'll play,
In the winter we won't.

All winter we sleep, each curled in a ball
As soon as the snowflakes start to fall.
But in spring we each come out of our den
And start to eat all over again.

Happy and Healthy

Eat Up, GEMMA

Written by Sarah Hayes

Illustrations by Jan Ormerod

One morning we woke up late.
I couldn't find my shoes
and Gemma wouldn't eat her breakfast.
"Eat up, Gemma," said Mom,
    but Gemma threw her breakfast on the floor.

45

46

Later on we went to the market.
Mom bought a bag of apples
and some bananas.
The man at the fruit stand
gave me a bunch of grapes.
He gave some to Gemma, too.
"Eat up, Gemma," said the man,
but Gemma pulled the
grapes off one by one
and squashed them.

When we got home
Grandma had made dinner.
"Nice and spicy," Dad said,
"just how I like it."
It was nice and spicy all right.
I drank three glasses of water.
"Eat up, Gemma," said Grandma.
Gemma banged her spoon on the table
and shouted.
But she didn't eat a thing.

50

The next day was Saturday
and Dad took us to the park.
We had chocolate cookies for a treat.
I ate two and then another two.
"Eat up, Gemma," said Dad.
But Gemma didn't eat her cookie.
She just licked off all the chocolate
and gave the rest to the birds.

In the evening our friends
were having a party.
"Eat up, everyone," said our friends.
And we did, all except Gemma.
    She sat on Grandma's knee
        and gave her dinner to the dog
            when Grandma wasn't looking.

53

After the party my friend came to stay
and we had a midnight feast.
Gemma didn't have any.
She was too tired.

In the morning we made Gemma a feast.
"Eat up, Gemma," said my friend.
Gemma picked up her toy hammer
and banged her feast to pieces.
My friend thought it was funny,
but Mom and Dad didn't.

57

Soon it was time for us to put on our
best clothes and go to church.
I sang very loudly.

The lady in front of us
had a hat with fruit on it.
I could see Gemma looking and looking.

When everyone was really quiet
Gemma leaned forward.
"Eat up, Gemma," she said.

Then she tried to pull
a grape off the lady's hat.
She pulled and pulled
and the lady's hat fell off.
Gemma hid her face in Dad's coat.

When we got home I had an idea.
I found a plate and a bowl.
I turned the bowl upside down
and put it on the plate.
Then I took a bunch of grapes
and two bananas and put them on the plate.
It looked just like the lady's hat.

64

"Eat up, Gemma," I said.
And she did.
She ate all the grapes
and the bananas.
She even tried to
eat the skins.

"Thank goodness for that," said Mom.
"We were getting worried," said Dad.
  Grandma smiled at me.
  I felt very proud.
"Gemma eat up," said Gemma,
  and we all laughed.

A Healthy Day

by Paul Showers

There are lots of things people do to stay healthy. You can do these things every day.

The food you eat every morning is important. Eating a good breakfast gets you ready for the day. It keeps your body from getting tired as you work and play.

68

All morning long, you're busy at home or school.
By lunchtime, your body begins to get tired.
Your body is telling you that it needs more food.

Fruit and Vegetable Group

69

At lunch and at every meal, it's a good idea to eat different kinds of foods. Milk gives you hard teeth and bones. Beans, peas, and fish help you grow. Carrots, corn, and potatoes give your body energy.

After a good lunch, you can play again without getting tired. Playing is good exercise, and your body needs exercise.

Exercise makes your bones and muscles get stronger.

71

There are many
ways to exercise.
You can skip rope
or do push-ups.
You can play games.
You can get lots
of exercise in games
like tag, baseball,
and basketball.

At the end of the day, just before bed, it's important to brush your teeth. Brushing your teeth keeps them clean and healthy. It also helps keep you from getting toothaches.

Sometimes, even when you eat good food, exercise, and brush your teeth, you may still get sick or have a toothache. Then, it's important to see a doctor or dentist. With their help and the things you do every day, you can make every day a healthy day.

Good Health to You!

by Paul Showers

I wrote A Healthy Day because good health is one of the most important things in the world.

You can't go to a store and buy it.

Nobody can give it to you as a present.

But to have good health, there are many things you can do. That's why I wrote my article — to tell you what those things are.

75

Looby Loo

Here we go looby loo,
Here we go looby light,
Here we go looby loo,
All on a Saturday night.

I put my right foot in,
I put my right foot out,
I give my right foot a shake, shake, shake,
And turn myself about.

Here we go looby loo,
Here we go looby light,
Here we go looby loo,
All on a Saturday night.

I put my left foot in,
I put my left foot out,
I give my left foot a shake, shake, shake,
And turn myself about.

This Tooth

by Lee Bennett Hopkins

I jiggled it
    jaggled it
    jerked it.

I pushed
    and pulled
    and poked it.

But —

As soon as I stopped,
and left it alone,
This tooth came out
on its very own!

Brave Dog

Story by Cynthia Rylant

Illustrations by
Suçie Stevenson

For lunch,
Henry and Mudge
and Henry's father
walked to a hot dog stand.

Henry had a hot dog
with ketchup.
Henry's father had a hot dog
with ketchup
and mustard
and onions
and slaw
and chili
and cheese.

"Yuck," said Henry.

Mudge had three hot dogs.
Plain.
In one gulp.

After lunch,
Henry and his father
began to build
a sand castle.

Henry made the moats.
Henry's father made the towers.
Mudge made a nice bed
and went to sleep.

When the castle was finished,
Henry's father
stuck his red rubber lobster
on the tallest tower.
Then he and Henry
clapped their hands.

Suddenly
a giant wave
washed far on the sand
and it covered everything.
It covered the moats.
It covered the towers.

It covered Mudge, who woke up.

"Oops," said Henry.

"Save that lobster!"
cried Henry's father.
The water was pulling it
out to sea.

Mudge ran and jumped
into the waves.
He caught the lobster
before it was lost forever.

"Good dog!" said Henry's father.
"Brave dog!" said Henry.
   They all had cherry sno-cones
   to celebrate.

AMAZING PETS

by Lynda DeWitt

Pets need people. Pets need us to give them food, water, and a place to sleep. People take care of their pets in many ways.

Did you know that sometimes pets help take care of people?

This dog leads a man through the park. The man cannot see. The dog takes him safely past benches and trees. The dog also helps the man cross streets.

This dog helps too. The woman cannot hear. The dog wakes the woman up when the alarm clock rings. The dog also lets the woman know when the doorbell rings.

Pets can do other amazing things. This monkey turns on the television for its owner. The owner cannot move his arms or legs. The monkey also turns on lights and opens doors.

These people are sick. Visiting with pets helps people feel better. They laugh at the funny things pets do. People love to talk to pets. People love to hold them. The animals love to be talked to and held too.

Pets are good friends. They can make us laugh. They can keep us from feeling lonely. Some pets can even be our eyes, our ears, and our hands.

The Lost Cat

by Shel Silverstein

We can't find the cat,
We don't know where she's at,
Oh, where did she go?
Does anyone know?
Let's ask this walking hat.

My Fish Can Ride a Bicycle

by Jack Prelutsky

My fish can ride a bicycle,
my fish can climb a tree,
my fish enjoys a glass of milk,
my fish takes naps with me.

My fish can play the clarinet,
my fish can bounce a ball,
my fish is not like other fish,
my fish can't swim at all.

Something Funny

PIZZA TIME

by James Marshall

Fox saw his friend Dexter
coming out of the pizza parlor.
"You can't fire *me*," said Dexter.
"I quit!"
"Fine," said the boss.
"Maybe my next delivery boy
won't eat up all the pizza!"
Dexter left in a huff.
And Fox stepped inside the
pizza parlor.

"Do you have a job for me?" asked Fox.
"Do you like pizza?" said the boss.
"I prefer hot dogs," said Fox.
"Excellent," said the boss.
"Are you fast on your feet?"

"Like the wind," said Fox.
"Excellent," said the boss.
"Take this pizza over to Mrs. O'Hara.
 She has been waiting a long time."
 Fox was out the door in a flash.

On Homer's Hill
Fox picked up speed.
"I'm the fastest fox in town,"
he said.
At that moment
Louise came around the corner.
She was taking her pet mice
to the vet for their shots.

It was quite a crash!
Fox, Louise, and everything else
went flying.
They saw stars.

"Now you've done it!" said Fox.
"You've made me late.
  I'll really have to step on it!"
  And he hurried away.

Louise went to the vet's.
Doctor Jane opened the box.
"Where are your pet mice?" she said.
"This looks like a pizza."
"Uh-oh," said Louise.

Fox knocked on Mrs. O'Hara's door.
"It's about time," said Mrs. O'Hara.
"I'm having a party.
  And we're just dying for pizza."
"It will be worth the wait," said Fox.

"Pizza time!"
said Mrs. O'Hara to her friends.
She opened the box.

Back at the pizza parlor
the boss was hopping mad.
"Mrs. O'Hara just called," he said.
"And you are fired!"
"Didn't she like the pizza?" said Fox.

DO YOUR EARS HANG LOW?

Do your ears hang low?
Do they wobble to and fro?
Can you tie them in a knot?
Can you tie them in a bow?
Can you throw them over your shoulder
Like a Continental soldier?
Do your ears hang low?

118

What is yellow,

has feathers,

up
and pops   and

down?

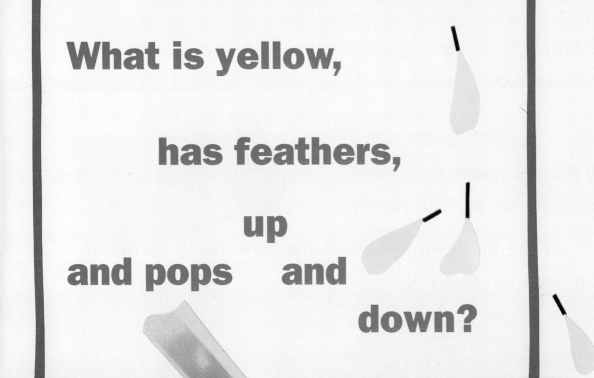

A canary with hiccups.

119

Books to Enjoy

How Many Teeth?

by Paul Showers

Illustrations by True Kelley

Out go the old teeth. In come the new. Read all about your teeth in this book.

The Mixed-Up Chameleon

by Eric Carle

An unhappy chameleon wishes for fins like a fish, a long neck like a giraffe, and a trunk like an elephant. But does this make him happy?

Five Silly Fishermen

by Roberta Edwards

Illustrations by Sylvie Wickstrom

Meet five silly fishermen who don't know how to count. So how will they know if one of them is missing?

120

The Bear Under the Stairs
by Helen Cooper

William is sure there's a scary
bear downstairs. Take a close
look to see if it's true.

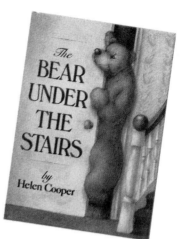

Henry and Mudge and the Happy Cat

by Cynthia Rylant
Illustrations by Suçie Stevenson

Henry and Mudge find a stray cat.
It's not cute. In fact, it looks like
mashed prunes. But they love it.

May We Sleep Here Tonight?
by Tan Koide
Illustrations by Yasuko Koide

Three gophers, two raccoons, and three rabbits
get lost in the fog. They find a house to sleep in.
Then, the owner of the house comes home!

Glossary

Words from your stories

Aa

ache

An **ache** is a pain or something that hurts. My arm **aches.** aches

Bb

bowl

A **bowl** is a deep dish. Jane ate a **bowl** of soup for lunch. **bowls**

bowl

brush

Brush means to clean, rub, or paint with a brush. **Brush** your teeth. **brushed, brushing**

cheese

Cc

cheese   **Cheese** is a food made from milk. **cheeses**

cover   When you **cover** something, you put something else over it. **covered, covering**

Dd

dentist   A **dentist** is a doctor who takes care of people's teeth. **dentists**

Ee

equal   The two dogs are **equal** in size. **equaled, equaling**

equal

123

exercise **Exercise** means to move the body to improve health. You **exercise** when you run, swim, or play ball.
exercised, exercising

exercise

Ff

feast A **feast** is a big meal for a special time. **feasts**

fire To be **fired** is to lose a job. **fired**

Gg

grape A **grape** is a small, round fruit. **Grapes** may be red, purple, or green. **grapes**

grapes

124

Hh

healthy   **Healthy** means to be in good health. **healthier, healthiest**

hear   I **hear** a knock at the door. **heard, hearing**

Ll

lobster   A **lobster** is an animal that lives in the ocean. **Lobsters** have hard shells. **lobsters**

lobster

lunch   **Lunch** is a meal eaten in the middle of the day. We had sandwiches for **lunch** today. **lunches**

125

Pp

piece   A **piece** is one of the parts into which something is divided. Kim cut the pie into **pieces.**
pieces

piece

Ss

stomach   The food you eat goes into your **stomach.** Your **stomach** is like a large bag inside your body.   **stomachs**

stomach

Tt

teeth   Your **teeth** help you bite and chew food.

126

tower   A **tower** is a tall building or part of a building. **towers**

tower

Vv

vet   **Vet** is another name for a veterinarian. A **vet** is a doctor who treats sick or injured animals. **vets**

Ww

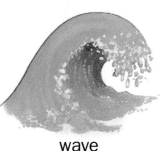

wave   When the water in an ocean or lake rises and moves forward, it forms a **wave. waves**

wave

wouldn't   **Wouldn't** means would not.

Acknowledgments

Text

Page 10: From *Two Greedy Bears* by Mirra Ginsburg, illustrated by Jose Aruego and Ariane Dewey. Copyright © 1976 by Mirra Ginsburg. Illustrations copyright © 1976 by Jose Aruego and Ariane Dewey. Reprinted by permission of Macmillan Publishing Company, a division of Macmillan, Inc.

Page 39: "Our Greedy Bears" by Jose Aruego and Ariane Dewey. Copyright © 1991 by Jose Aruego and Ariane Dewey.

Page 40: "Polar Bear" by Gail Kredenser Mack. Reprinted by permission of Gail Kredenser Mack.

Page 41: "In the Summer We Eat" from *Bits and Pieces* by Zhenya Gay. Copyright © 1958 by Zhenya Gay, renewed © 1986 by Erika L. Hinchley. Used by permission of Viking Penguin, a division of Penguin Books USA Inc.

Page 44: *Eat Up, Gemma* written by Sarah Hayes. Illustrated by Jan Ormerod. Text copyright © 1988 by Sarah Hayes. Illustrations copyright © 1988 by Jan Ormerod. Published by Lothrop, Lee & Shepard Books, a Division of William Morrow & Company, Inc. Reprinted by permission of William Morrow & Company, Inc. and Walker Books Limited.

Page 68: *A Healthy Day* by Paul Showers. Copyright © 1991 by Paul Showers.

Page 75: "Good Health to You!" by Paul Showers. Copyright © 1991 by Paul Showers.

Page 80: "This Tooth" from *More Surprises* by Lee Bennett Hopkins. Text copyright © 1987 by Lee Bennett Hopkins. Reprinted by permission of HarperCollins Publishers.

Page 84: "Brave Dog." Reprinted with the permission of Simon & Schuster Books for Young Readers from *Henry and Mudge and the Forever Sea* by Cynthia Rylant, illustrated by Sucie Stevenson. Text copyright © 1989 by Cynthia Rylant. Illustrations copyright © 1989 by Sucie Stevenson.

Page 96: *Amazing Pets* by Lynda DeWitt. Copyright © 1991 by Lynda DeWitt.

Page 102: "The Lost Cat" text and art from *A Light in the Attic* by Shel Silverstein. Copyright © 1981 by Evil Eye Music, Inc. Reprinted by permission of HarperCollins Publishers.

Page 103: "My Fish Can Ride a Bicycle" from *Something Big Has Been Here,* poems by Jack Prelutsky, drawings by James Stevenson. Text copyright © 1990 by Jack Prelutsky. Illustrations copyright © 1990 by James Stevenson. Published by Greenwillow Books, a Division of William Morrow & Company, Inc. Reprinted by permission of William Morrow & Company, Inc.

Page 106: "Pizza Time" from *Fox on the Job* by James Marshall. Copyright © 1988 by James Marshall. Used by permission of Dial Books for Young Readers, a division of Penguin Books USA Inc.

Page 119: Riddle from *Ready. . .Set. . .Read!* by Joanna Cole and Stephanie Calmenson. Reprinted by permission of Stephanie Calmenson.

Artists

Illustrations owned and copyrighted by the illustrator.
Michele Noiset, cover, 1–9, 42–43, 82–83, 104–105, 120–127
Jose Aruego and Ariane Dewey, 10–39
Kevin Hawkes, 40
Lonni Sue Johnson, 41
Jan Ormerod, 44–67
Lee Tracy, 76–79
Myron Grossman, 81
Sucie Stevenson, 84–95
Janice Skivington, 96–101
Shel Silverstein, 102
James Stevenson, 103
James Marshall, 106–117
Lois Ehlert, 118–119

Freelance Photography

Photographs not listed were shot by Scott, Foresman and Company.

Photographs

Page 39: Courtesy of Jose Aruego and Ariane Dewey.
Page 75: Courtesy of Paul Showers.

Glossary

The contents of the Glossary have been adapted from *My First Picture Dictionary,* copyright © 1990 Scott, Foresman and Company; *My Second Picture Dictionary,* copyright © 1990 Scott, Foresman and Company; and *Beginning Dictionary,* copyright © 1993 Scott, Foresman and Company.